Priscilla's Lost & Found

George and Linda B

All images are either the author's or a composite of contributions from Pixabay. Pixabay is a Creative Commons source, and all are copyright-free. Significant contributing Pixabay artists from whom most of the main characters and visuals were created are as follows: susannp4 (Priscilla, mushrooms, and other items), prosaica (Civil War Scene), Shared Design (Gold Medal), geralt (explosion), yokim (young Hattie), DeeDee51 (King Gregory and wildflowers), Jazella (throne and mushrooms), truthseeker08 (hand), Chippyri (worm), MiM326 (fire), denisejhills (net), HUNGQUACH679PNG (white dove), CoolCatGamesStudio (gold valuables), mk_graphics (gold coins), MLARANDA (raven's head), Parker-West (stone throne), jjuni (eye glasses broken), thefairypath (ballroom), annie1loves1you (Hattie's crown), carocta (underground background), pendleburyannette (the tiny white-headed bird man, Wanda, and others), SilviaP Design (nymph warriors), Ractapopulous (nymph warriors), LOSTMIND (Dora's Victorian house), Anaterate (Cilla's grandfather, moles, elder's beard and others), AILes (hats, pocket watch), KaosShots (books), janastart (Great Uncle Jim), sinousxl, Mohamed_hassan, 1820796 (Olie Owl), Buntysmum (tree leaves), OpenClpart-Vector (Fredrick's hat, hammers, grub, root, glasses).

Note: In addition to the above contributions, there could be other Pixabay pieces that were used; however, my photography, images, and creative recombination comprise the majority. On Pixabay, where I have published over 2,000 images, my identification is GeorgeB2. My photos and images have been viewed over one million times and downloaded for copyright-free use over half a million times.

ISBN (Paperback): 979-8-9894070-8-8
ISBN (Hardcover): 979-8-9894070-9-5
ISBN (eBook): 979-8-9894070-7-1

Priscilla's Lost and Found

Pride and Anger versus Forgiveness

Priscilla's grandfather's youngest brother, Jim, lost his pocket watch while he was visiting his brother Henry Smyth, his niece Dora, and his grandniece Priscilla.

The gold watch was carried by his father during the Civil War and was Jim's most prized possession. It was the only thing he owned that was his father's. Henry, Priscilla's grandfather, and his youngest brother Jim looked everywhere but were unable to find the lost and priceless heirloom.

Priscilla, understanding the importance of the lost watch, decided to help him find his prized possession. Jim was sure he had it when he was in the yard looking at the pond with Henry. When they discovered the loss some hours after it happened, Henry and Jim thoroughly searched the area around the yard and pond but to their frustration they found nothing. It was like it vanished from the earth.

Priscilla knew her yard friends would have some ideas about what happened and decided to enlist their help to find the pocket watch. Priscilla, Cilla for short, had come to live with her Aunt Dora and Grandfather Henry Smyth several months before due to the loss of her family to the Spanish flu. She is now a full member of her new family and wanted very badly to help in any way she could.

Sid, the little man in charge of the bird rider flight academy, and all the yard friends agreed to help Priscilla. They did a thorough search but found nothing, except for a lost pair of reading glasses. However, they were suspicious of the Ravens. The pesky birds were known for picking up bright and shiny objects. They would take them to their mates trying to impress them with their finds.

They suggested Priscilla talk to the flock master, Sammie. He could be found with his mate in the yard down the road about a mile away. They often raided Cilla's yard for prizes especially when Malcolm Hawk (the yard protector) was away from the yard. So that is exactly what Cilla did; she got Sid to shrink her so she could fly on Ollie Owl to talk to Sammie.

After Priscilla explained why she came to talk, Sammie the Flock Master responded, "Sammie says, Sammie says, Sammie says; we found the watch, the watch, the watch. We dropped the watch, we dropped, we dropped, we dropped it. Went into a hole near the pond, the pond, the pond. A hole, a hole, a hole. It is gone, gone, gone!"

"Thank you, Flock Master Sammie." Cilla pleads, "Please show me the hole."

"Yes, we can show you the hole, the hole, hole, hole. But the moles, moles, moles must have it by now, now, now.'"

After Cilla tells her friends what Sammie told her, they inform her that it is common knowledge that the Mole kingdom is where all lost objects eventually end up. Also, the Mole kingdom is not visited by the yard friends.

They tell her the moles rule the underground and they collect and hoard all the items they find. They only come out during the night so she will have to seek them out after dark. However, even if they admit they have something, they will not give it back unless you give them something in return.

Sid, advises Cilla not to go underground but if she insists, he agrees to shrink her so she can search for the watch.

However, Priscilla is determined to find her family's watch and decides to try to contact the reclusive creatures.

Cilla asks everyone she knows in the yard about the moles however, everyone says the same thing. They know they exist and there is a strange kind of war between them and the people on the surface, but they know no more than that.

Priscilla reads about moles from books in her grandfather's library. She discovers the moles are very mysterious creatures and live underground except for brief periods when they might be seen when their burrows become uncovered accidentally. They eat grubs and worms and use venom to paralyze their prey so they can collect and store them in one place.

During the day, Cilla goes to the mole hole Sammie showed her and looks in. She puts her hand in to see how deep she can go. She feels nothing but catches sight of a gleaming object way down. She suspects the object is the watch but is upset because she cannot reach it.

Priscilla thinks she knows where the watch is and goes to Sid to get him to shrink her; however, she wants to wait for nightfall because the Mole People are more active at night.

Sid reluctantly gives Cilla magic words she can use to shrink herself; as well as a command to return to her normal size. All she needs to do to shrink is close her eyes and repeat the following words. *I shrink myself; I shrink myself; I shrink myself.* To return to normal size she opens her eyes and repeats the following words . . . *I grow, grow, grow.* With these words, Cilla can shrink and enlarge as she chooses, and all without the help of Sid.

The good thing is, Cilla can act independently, the bad thing is if she does act on her own, Sid and others may not be there to help her if something goes wrong.

Later that evening, Priscilla shrinks herself using the words Sid gave her. She then plans to explore the Mole kingdom. So, that is just what she does alone against the advice of her friends. As one might predict, she trips over a stone around the edge of the hole and falls headfirst down into the darkness.

Once Priscilla hits the bottom, the watch is nowhere to be found and she begins to look further. She starts to explore and runs into Willie Mole.

He is friendly but eccentric, Priscilla asks Willie, "Can you help me find my family's watch?"

He says, "I will help you if you help us. You see everything we find is ours . . . finders, keepers, losers, weepers; that is our way of life."

Cilla complains," Don't you do anything just to be nice, what if you lost something of value to you?"

Willie snorts, "No one talks to us unless they want something, so why should we be nice? They call us strange, ugly, blind, and dirty because we tunnel through the dirt. We live and go where others can't, we paralyze our food with venom and eat worms and other strange things. We live on very little air; we breathe where others cannot. Your yard friends want nothing to do with us."

Priscilla asserts, "I am talking to you now, I don't think you are ugly and I would like to be your friend, how can I help you? I am usually good at solving problems."

Willie thinks for a moment, *Hmmm, if this creature can help the sleeping Princess, then we might be able to help her.*

Willie agrees, "OK, let me show you around!"

Priscilla announces, "My real name is Priscilla, but my friends call me Cilla."

Willie leads Cilla through the molehill into the deeper recesses of the tunnels. The walls glow with a low blue and green light and Cilla's eyes adjust to the dim surroundings. There are larger and larger chambers connecting several exits and entrances. Eventually, they come to one very large space with a good-sized room that glows yellow. To her surprise, the room is full of gold!

Willie notices Cilla's surprise and interjects," Yes, it is gold; this collection is all the valuable objects we find lost from your world above. This pile is old. You can see it is impressive. We are wealthy, yet we don't use our wealth, we just keep collecting gold and it ends up in here."

Cilla asks; "Do you have a ruler or a government that runs your kingdom?"

Willie slowly admits, "Sort of. We have a Master Blacksmith (Fredrick Wise Mole), he has not really ruled since he was cheated out of his rightful compensation by King Gregory. He worked hard to make a crown for Princess Hattie. The same crown the Princess wears right now in our treasure room. It is a long story. You see Hattie has been asleep since I was born. Would you like to see her?"

Priscilla enthusiastically agrees, "Sure!"

Willie leads the guest from the surface world to the other side of the room. There sitting on a stone throne is a young girl dressed in regal clothes sitting still without moving, slowly breathing, eyes closed. To Priscilla, she looked like she was in her late teens, possibly seventeen.

Cilla inquired, "Has anyone tried to wake her up?"

"Oh, no!" Willie warned, "The Master Blacksmith told us never to disturb her. He keeps her in this state through his paralyzing venom. We just watch and keep putting gold in the room. Fredrick says he might wake her up when we have collected enough treasure."

Priscilla asks if there is anyone else who might know more about the Princess. Willie said there was an elder mole who might know. He once helped the Master Blacksmith. He made beautiful things for people on the surface for pay. However, since the Princess has been asleep, he has not worked.

The Magic Kingdom
In Priscilla's Yard

When Willie took Priscilla to the elder, he told her that long before the enormous house on the surface existed, there was an ancient kingdom.

This kingdom was ruled by a King who had a young daughter whose name was Hattie. Hattie had abilities no other person had. She was strong-willed; she could stop anyone from harming herself or others. However, she was self-centered and selfish just like her father, and never smiled.

Even as a young child, Hattie was quick to take offense to unwanted words or actions from others. One terrible day when Princess Hattie was seventeen, she was kidnapped, and the King could not understand how this could happen due to her abilities. Not only was she taken but after many years he was unable to secure her return.

You see the kidnappers were thought to be us, the Mole People. Since we live underground and are very mysterious, we became greatly feared and mistrusted after Hattie's disappearance.

Let's go back to the beginning. When Hattie was thirteen, King Gregory wanted a crown made so his family and all future Princesses would have a special emblem to show their pride. He understood we were experts in crafting such a special item. So, he sent out word for the Master Blacksmith from our realm to make the best crown possible.

The King asked Fredrick Wise Mole to make the crown and sent half of the reward for his efforts and agreed to pay the rest when the crown was finished.

Fredrick accepted the initial payment and verbally agreed to make this crown and spent months on the effort.

Once completed Fredrick sent the crown to King Gregory for his review and approval, expecting the rest of his payment.

The Master Craftsman used tiny white jewels. King Gregory wanted large blue stones but had not made this clear to Fredrick.

We understand the more Gregory thought about the jewels he wanted the angrier he got. The prideful King refused to admit he was wrong and chose to keep the crown without paying Fredrick the full amount he had promised. He gave it to Hattie as a birthday present and she wore it every day thereafter, even when she slept.

Neither King Gregory nor Fredrick Wise Mole had made their choices known to each other and both claimed they had done so. Then their pride took over. Each refused to compromise. The King refused to pay, and the Master Blacksmith demanded full payment and did not even offer to change the stones in the crown.

If Fredrick Wise Mole could not get the gold, he felt he was owed, he wanted revenge. He plotted to get the crown back no matter what he had to do or how long it took to accomplish his goal. His pride and anger led directly to Hattie's abduction.

His anger grew because on the surface, the people refused to discuss his complaint. The pride of both parties turned our people underground and those creatures on the surface from friendly cooperation into a running battle.

Then one fateful day when Hattie was seventeen, we captured her. Fredrick thought we could just take her crown and release her. In no way did we want to keep Hattie. However, to our surprise, we could not get the crown from her. She had the power to prevent us from taking the crown but not the power to escape. We think her anger caused her magical powers to be partially unusable.

When prideful Hattie refused to give up her crown in exchange for her freedom, Fredrick injected his venom into her, and she fell asleep and remains asleep until this day."

On hearing the whole story, Cilla thought how tragic it all was. She decided to try to get the Princess freed if she could.

She prayed for an answer and Priscilla was told forgiveness was the key to fixing the situation. Forgiving others first for their wrongdoing was the answer. Priscilla was told the Princess must first truly forgive Fredrick Wise Mole for abducting her. If she did so, everything would flow correctly from her unselfish act.

So, Priscilla got in front of the sleeping girl, placed her hands on her hands, and repeated. "Open your eyes dear one, open your eyes, open your eyes, open your eyes; your freedom awaits."

Hattie awoke startled, and angry. She asked who Priscilla was and where they were. Cilla explained what had happened. The Princess started to sob when she remembered the events that happened just before she was put to sleep.

Cilla warned her not to turn to anger and stubbornly hold on to the cursed crown, she must forgive the past or there would be no future.

The Princess went quiet for a long time but finally spoke. As she talked, she removed the crown from her head.

Hattie calmly declared, "This crown is not worth my freedom, I wish to go on with my life and forgive the past. Please give this crown to Fredrick Wise Mole. If he frees me, I will ask my father to forgive the past as well. The inability to forgive has almost destroyed my life and others, it is over."

When Fredrick heard Hattie was awake and voluntarily gave up the crown, he felt very ashamed.

His heart melted and he forgave the Princess and her father. He not only freed the Princess but gave her back the crown. His need for revenge was gone. He realized his inability to forgive had made his life and those around him lonely and outcasts. Hattie's forgiveness allowed him to see clearly that he was wrong. He sent word to King Gregory of his actions; he not only sent Hattie home but sent the crown as well.

King Gregory an old man now smiled (the King that never smiled); because he was so happy to know that his daughter was coming home. For the first time, the crown meant nothing to him.

His need to withhold payment was now silly to him. He sent the Master Mole every gold thing he owned in payment for the crown. He vowed never to let anger and non-forgiveness control his actions ever again.

When Fredrick Wise Mole heard what Priscilla did and found out about the watch she was seeking, he ordered his people to find the prized possession and anything else she wanted.

The Mole People gleefully brought the watch to the surface and waited for Priscilla to come and get it.

The brave young girl took possession of the watch from the moles and told her family she had a surprise for them.

Priscilla presented the recovered watch to her grandfather.

Her grandfather then returned the honored possession to his younger brother. Grandfather Smyth asked, "How in the world did you find the pocket watch?"

Priscilla explained, "It was a group effort, and I could not have gotten the watch back without divine help and support from all my yard friends." She explained the task was very complicated and she would one day explain it when everyone had plenty of time to listen.

One day Cilla would tell her family that Princess Hattie was willing to forgive first. Her forgiveness led directly to her father and Fredrick Wise Mole resolving a long and bitter conflict that hurt many people.

Hattie started the chain reaction by which everyone forgave each other, the Mole People found new relationships with the surface creatures, King Gregory got back his daughter, and all sides received amazing results when they dared to forgive.

The End

About the Authors

The author George B is an avid photographer and graphic designer. He retired as a senior scientist and shares his writing passion with his wife of forty-four years.

Linda B, the coauthor, is a teacher, registered nurse, and an accomplished musician. She teaches piano and plays for churches.

Our creative efforts are found in three previous children's books, *Priscilla's Prayer*, *Priscilla's Angels, Priscilla's Miracle,* and now, in our fourth children's book *Priscilla's Lost and Found*. We have published two previous books written for older audiences: *Struggle and Survival a Boneyard Saga, Short Story Anthology,* and *Volume 1, Mona Lisa on the Moon, Thirty-Two Thousand Years in the Making*.

Lost and Found Book Dedication

This book is dedicated to all the families and friends who have dared to forgive. Those brave souls who embrace forgiveness in the place of rage, mistrust, stubbornness, and being offended or disrespected. Please discover before it is too late that possessions, property, money, or hurt feelings can never replace a dear friend or family.

www.ingramcontent.com/pod-product-compliance
Lightning Source LLC
LaVergne TN
LVHW070535070526
838199LV00075B/6782